Understanding and Caring for Your Pet

Cats

MC

Understanding and Caring for Your Pet

Written by
Claire Horton-Bussey

Mason Crest
450 Parkway Drive, Suite D
Broomall, PA 19008
www.masoncrest.com
Developed and produced by Mason Crest

Printed and bound in the United States of America.

First printing
9 8 7 6 5 4 3 2 1

Series ISBN: 978-1-4222-3691-8
ISBN: 978-1-4222-3693-2
ebook ISBN: 978-1-4222-8085-0

Every reasonable care has been taken in the compilation of this publication.
The Publisher and Author cannot accept liability for any loss, damage, injury, or death
resulting from the keeping of cats by user(s) of this publication, or from the use of
any materials, equipment, methods, or information recommended in this publication
or from any errors or omissions that may be found in the text of this publication or
that may occur at a future date, except as expressly provided by law. No animals were
harmed in the making of this book.

Words in bold are explained in the glossary on page 127.

QR CODES AND LINKS TO THIRD PARTY CONTENT

You may gain access to certain third party content ("Third Party Sites") by scanning
and using the QR Codes that appear in this publication (the "QR Codes"). We do not
operate or control in any respect any information, products or services on such Third
Party Sites linked to by us via the QR Codes included in this publication, and we
assume no responsibility for any materials you may access using the QR Codes. Your
use of the QR Codes may be subject to terms, limitations, or restrictions set forth
in the applicable terms of use or otherwise established by the owners of the Third
Party Sites. Our linking to such Third Party Sites via the QR Codes does not imply an
endorsement or sponsorship of such Third Party Sites, or the information, products or
services offered on or through the Third Party Sites, nor does it imply an endorsement
or sponsorship of this publication by the owners of such Third Party Sites.

Understanding and Caring for Your Pet

Aquarium
Cats
Dog Training
Ferrets
Gerbils
Goldfish

Guinea Pigs
Hamsters
Kittens
Parakeets
Puppies
Rabbits

 Educational Videos: Readers can view videos by scanning our QR codes, providing them with additional educational content to supplement the text. Examples include news coverage, moments in history, speeches, iconic moments, and much more!

 Words to Understand: These words with their easy-to-understand definitions will increase the reader's understanding of the text, while building vocabulary skills.

Contents

Introduction

Cats are one of the most popular pets in the world, and it's easy to understand why. They are ideal for modern-living, requiring little money, space, or training, compared to many pets, and, of course, they are incredibly adaptable, thriving in all sorts of households—single homes, busy families, older couples, country or town, apartment or mansion. Provided he is safe from roads and other dangers and can have his basic care needs met, a cat will make himself at home in many types of living arrangements.

Unlike dogs, cats can be left for hours while their owners work. They are small and do not require a large home or yard. In fact, a cat can be perfectly content spending his whole life indoors.

Of course, cats can't just lie around doing nothing all the time. They must have adequate opportunities to express their natural behaviors (hunting, climbing, scratching, etc.) indoors.

Size also works in the cat's favor. They don't require large homes or yards, they can be picked up and carried easily, are easy to take to the vet, they don't require huge bowls of food, and they fit on a lap perfectly well for a cuddle!

They come in many colors and patterns, and, for those who would like even further choice, there are many **pedigree** breeds from which to choose, too. There really is a cat for almost every taste!

Taming the Wild Cat

Watch a cat playing in the yard or stalking a toy on the rug and it's not difficult to see where his origins lie. He may have been domesticated for several thousand years, but he still retains many features of his wild ancestor, the African wildcat.

The cat family (Felidae) is a varied group, and emerged during the Miocene period, which was about 10 million to 11 million years ago. These feline ancestors eventually evolved into eight major groups, including the Panthera (lions, tiger, and other big cats), and Felis (smaller wildcats).

The story of the domesticated cat (*Felis silvestris catus*) began with the agricultural revolution about 10,000 to 12,000 years ago, when humans began storing their crops. Rats and mice posed a serious threat to the stores, and a pack of rats could mean starvation for the humans. Fortunately, cats were equally as attracted to the granaries—not for the grain but for the easy rodent hunting! People welcomed the cats' help in getting rid of the rodents, and, over time, the cats became less fearful of humans and relaxed around the human settlements.

A combination of some kind of genetic mutation occurring, together with selective breeding (with the people-tolerant cats in the settlement mating with others of a similar character), meant the cat became domesticated over time. About 4,000 years ago, the Egyptians began domesticating cats more seriously, and keeping them as pets.

His fortunes have waxed and waned through the ages, from being worshipped in Ancient Egypt to being persecuted in the Middle Ages because of an association with witches, but he is now securely at the top of our list of favorite pets.

How Many?

It's often said that cats are solitary creatures, but this isn't true. Yes, cats are solitary hunters, unlike some animals that hunt in pairs or packs, but they often choose to live happily in groups. This is evident from watching feral cat groups, where close, lasting relationships can be seen, particularly in the adult females, who help to nurse and raise kittens together.

An only cat in a home will be more than content, provided his needs are met, but many cats can—and do—live happily with one or more of their own kind. The key to success is to make both cats are sociable and have similar activity levels, and that each individual's needs are met (that they each receive plenty of petting, lap-warming, play, and quiet time alone, where they can escape to a snooze spot away from others if they want to).

Most squabbles arise over competition for resources. So make sure that each cat has their own litter box, bed, food, and water bowl, and perch (somewhere such as a high windowsill). Remember, you also count as a resource, so make sure you give your lap and attention to each cat, too!

Personality also plays a part, of course. Some cats are simply loners and only you will know if your cat would accept a newcomer. Perhaps you have a senior who has never shared his home with a feline friend and is aggressive to any cat that strays into the yard. Maybe you have a younger, very territorial cat or one who is very nervous and fearful. Such cats are generally in the minority, however. Most will accept a new cat in the home, provided the situation is handled carefully.

- Scent is an important part of cat communication. Stroke one cat and then the other, rubbing under the cat's chin and his 'cheeks' at the sides of his mouth. Your hand will transfer the smell from his scent glands to the other cat. When they meet in the flesh, they will already be familiar with each other's scent.

- If you fear they could become aggressive or chase each other, use a cat carrier to house the newcomer for the initial introductions, so they can get used to each other without any risk of harm.

- Introduce them before a meal-time, so they are hungry and easily distracted by food. Feed them in the same room but a good distance away from each other, so they don't feel threatened.

- Remain calm so the cats don't pick up any anxiety from you.

- Repeat the introductions often, keeping it short and sweet until they are quite comfortable with each other. When you can't supervise, keep the cats in separate rooms.

- Have some tasty treats to hand, such as slices of hotdog or diced chicken, and reward any calm behavior.

With time, they will become increasingly confident around each other, and, in many cases, will be curling up next to each other for a nap before you know it!

Where to Get Your Cat

Where to Get Your Cat

The best place to find an adult cat is from a reputable rescue group or shelter. Here you will find a good selection of cats—perhaps even a pedigree—who have been vet-checked and handled and assessed by experienced staff. There are many types of rescue groups. Some find new homes for dogs and cats (and sometimes rabbits and other small pets, too), some just specialize in cats, and some are dedicated to just one breed, such as the Siamese.

If you want a rescue cat of a particular breed, you may have to wait some time for the right cat to become available, especially in the numerically small breeds, but if you would like a mixed breed, you will have plenty of cats to choose from.

Shelters and rescue groups are usually crowded with beautiful cats of every description. Some may be there because they have strayed and cannot be reunited with their owners, and some may be given up for rehoming because of a change in their owners' circumstances (such as moving to non-cat-friendly accommodation, death, or illness).

If the cat has been handed in by the previous owner, you will know his full history. This is a great advantage in finding the right cat for your home and lifestyle. For example, if you have a dog and/or children, you can choose a puss who has previously lived happily with a canine and youngsters.

Where a cat's history isn't known—the case of a stray, for example—staff will assess him and place him accordingly. Some large centers have consultant behaviorists who can iron out any issues before rehoming, and all organizations should offer post-adoption support and advice if you have any questions or problems.

Every rescue group has its own policies, but you will generally be interviewed, to assess your family and home's suitability and to find out your wants and needs. You may be asked for personal references, and a veterinarian as a reference as well.

Most rescue groups collect an adoption fee to cover the expenses incurred of neutering the cat, worming, flea treatments, and any other vet fees. This adoption fee is typically much lower than what you would pay for all these services.

Preparing
Your Home

Preparing Your Home

Before bringing your adult cat home, it's important that you prepare a room that puss can call his own. Your bedroom is ideal. Cats, when stressed, seek small hiding places where they can feel safe and protected. Introducing him to your entire home and expecting him to settle in right away is asking too much. First, get him used to one room and then, as he gains confidence, he will venture out and start exploring the rest of the house in his own time, returning to his "safe room" if spooked.

Preparing your home
for a new cat

Place his bed, litter box, and food and water bowls in the room, making sure that the litter box is as far away from the bed and bowls as it can be (nobody likes to go to the toilet where they eat!). Put some toys in the room for him to play with (or for you to play with together when you visit the room), and also put a scratching post inside. Make sure the windows are locked (some smart cats can open windows!) and make sure the room is cat-safe (no **toxic** houseplants, such as poinsettia or lilies; no irreplaceable heirlooms on a mantelpiece or shelf within the cat's reach, etc).

Next, cat-proof the rest of the house and yard. Assess each room from a cat's perspective, getting down on all fours if necessary! Put breakable ornaments away or display them in a glass-fronted cabinet, and remove or put out of reach any toxic plants. Adult cats aren't usually as manic as kittens, who seem genetically programd to find dangling wires to play   with and chew, but some cats seem determined to find trouble wherever they are, so it's better to be safe than sorry; gather up excess electrical wire and fasten with a cable tie.

You should also discuss with all family members some basic rules to make sure the new cat's safety:

- The toilet seat should always be put down when not in use, so a curious puss can't jump in and/or drink from the bowl and ingest any harmful chemicals.

- Windows should be shut/locked and doors kept closed Screens can be fitted to windows that allow air to enter, but prevent a cat escaping.

- The washing machine and dryer doors should be kept shut when not in use and the insides should be checked before they are switched on in case puss has crept inside. All chemicals and medicines should be shut away (antifreeze, aspirin, and acetaminophen, for example, can be deadly to cats).

- The shed/garage should always be checked before being locked up, in case your cat has sneaked inside.

- Only use products that are entirely cat-safe in your yard and garden.

- If you have a pool or pond, these should be covered and ramps should be fitted so that your cat can climb out if he falls in. As part of your preparations, you should also fit a catflap to the back door (unless you want to be pestered relentlessly to let the cat out and in and out again...) and set it to the locked position so your new puss can't yet escape into the big, wide world.

If you have a dog in your home, fit a baby gate so your cat can have his safe room to himself, away from any canine attention. In time, and with careful introductions, he will be happy to slip through the gate and be social, but in the early days, he will want to find his feet and settle in, unbothered by the family dog.

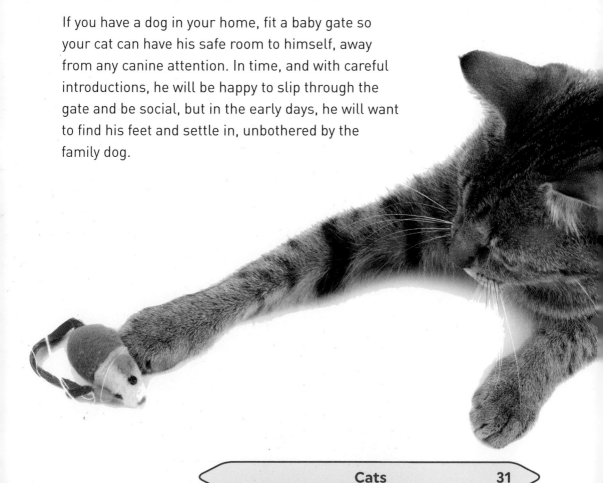

Essential
Equipment

Essential equipment

A cat's needs are pretty basic compared to some pets, but there are some essential things you should shop for before bringing him home.

Essential equipment for cat owners

Bed

There is a bed to suit every taste and budget. Although you can get ornate four-posters and sofa longues for cats (yes, really!), most have humbler tastes, preferring a pile of freshly washed laundry! A simple, fleecy pad-type bed is a good starting point, or, better still, a hooded cat bed, which will help to make puss feel safe and protected. Place the bed in a corner of the room, or, if it is deep enough, on a windowsill.

Bowls

You will need at least two bowls—one for food and one for water—though four are ideal, so you have one being washed while another set is being used. Choose from glass, ceramic, or stainless steel. Avoid plastic bowls, which can eventually scratch and become quite abrasive. The design is important: cats prefer to eat from shallow bowls rather than deep ones.

Food

Find out in advance what the cat is fed so you can get a supply before you bring him home. Most rescue groups will feed whatever has been donated, but some cats may have specific food whims. Cats are known for being fussy—if you let them!

Litter Accessories

You will need a litter box, scoop, a place to dispose of what you scoop, cat-safe cleaner (unscented dish detergent works well for cleaning the box), and a supply of cat litter. Even a cat who spends some time outside needs a litter box for when he is inside and has to go.

If you already have a cat, get another box for the newcomer, because many cats will not use a box that is used by another cat. The general rule is as many boxes as there are cats, plus one—so two cats will need three boxes between them.

Get the biggest litter box available. Most boxes are too small, so go for jumbo. Some cats prefer the privacy that a covered box offers, while others can feel claustrophobic and prefer an open box. Bear in mind that the best way of keeping a sweet-smelling home is to scoop twice a day and change the litter regularly— whether the box has a cover or not. If the litter is very dirty, most self-respecting cats won't use it and will find a clean corner of the house to relieve themselves instead!

There are many types of litter—wood-based pellets, paper, clay, silica crystals, lightweight, and the clumping type that forms a scoopable clump when it comes into contact with liquid. Find out what your cat is used to and get a supply before bringing him home.

If you want to change the type of litter, add a little of the new stuff to the one he's used to already, mix it in, and gradually, over the course of a few days increase the amount of new to old until the change is complete.

Litter
be filled
inches dee
of course, cha
twice a day.

Identification

Most shelters will microchip the cats in their care before they are rehomed, but if you get your cat from another source, then you may have to arrange for your vet to do it. It is a simple procedure where a small chip, the size of a long grain of rice, is inserted under the skin at the back of the neck, between the shoulder blades. This chip contains a unique number, which will be held in a database with your details. If your cat becomes lost and is scanned by a reader, you can quickly be reunited. Occasionally, chips fail, so it is worth asking your vet to scan your cat at his annual check-up, to make sure it is still working properly. But the failure rate is very low and chipping has proved to be a very easy, reliable form of identification.

In addition, a collar and tag is useful so your cat can be returned to you without a scanner, and if it is made of reflective material, it could help improve your cat's visibility in low light.

It is very important that the collar is a safe one and will not strangle your cat if it is caught on a branch or something similar. A safety-clip, breakaway collar that snaps open under pressure is a good option.

Scratching post

Scratching is an important part of feline behavior. Expecting a cat not to scratch is entirely unreasonable, but scratching needn't be a problem—as long as you provide your cat with suitable places to perform the behavior. If he has a scratching post that is the right material, at the right height, and in the right position (see page 75), then he'll have no need to put his claws anywhere near your new sofa. Two or three posts should be sufficient for most homes, but you may need more if you have more cats.

Avoid carpet-covered scratching boards and posts— your cat might associate the material with the action and then begin scratching your floor coverings. Sisal is therefore preferable.

Toys

A good selection of toys is a worthwhile investment. If you spend time regularly playing with your cat, you will not only strengthen your relationship, but you'll also be helping to keep him active and stimulated (if bored, he might seek amusement by climbing your curtains, "hunting" your shoelaces etc). Plus, playing with a cat is simply great fun and a fabulous way of de-stressing!

The range of toys available these days is astonishing, with everything from fishing-rod type toys and balls with bells to remote-controlled mice and multi-toy activity centers. There is something to suit every puss—and purse!

Whatever toys you buy, don't make every one constantly available to your cat. To keep his interest in them, put them away, and bring out a couple every day for him to play with. The next day, swap them with different toys. Rotating his toys will help to retain their novelty value for longer.

Also remember that toys don't play by themselves. Giving him a toy mouse might amuse him for a few minutes, but he'll soon lose interest if it's not wiggled to attract his attention, or thrown for him to chase and "hunt."

Feliway

Scent is very important to cats, not only as a means of communication to other cats but also in terms of a cat's personal sense of security. If a home smells of his own scent, he will feel far safer than in a new home where there are unfamiliar scents. Cats put their own smells on objects by rubbing their scent glands against them, particularly facial glands. This is why a cat will rub his head against the side of furniture, your legs, or against your hand while he is being petted.

Before you bring your new puss home, put a **pheromone** diffuser (Feliway) in his room, and leave it on continuously for at least four weeks after he arrives. This will reassure him and really help him to feel secure and "at home."

Behavior

Behavior

Body language

The cat has lived alongside human beings for thousands of years and knows perfectly well how to make his feelings known to us. You don't have to be a behaviorist to realize that when a cat is hissing, with his fur on end and his back arched, that he doesn't want to be stroked right now! Or that if he is purring loudly, eyes half-closed, and rolling on his back, rubbing against you, that he is enjoying being petted!

Cat behavior—why they do what they do.

But there are some surprises. For example, a cat doesn't always purr from pleasure—it can also be a sign that he is in pain. Many injured cats or those giving birth will purr, as will dying cats.

Tail

A cat uses his tail for balance when climbing and cornering at speed, and also to communicate. The tail will generally be held horizontally or slightly lower, but will be raised upright as a signal of a friendly greeting.

If he wags his tail, it's generally a sign of agitation, or milder irritation if it's just the tip that is flicking.

Fur

A cat will fluff up his fur (known as piloerection) to make himself look bigger and fiercer. He also does it, to a lesser extent, when he's cold, with the hair trapping air against the skin. A cat's piloerection is similar to our own: we get goosebumps, with our body hair standing on end when we're cold or spooked, too!

Eyes

If a cat gives you a long, slow blink, it's usually a sign that he is very content and relaxed. By contrast, an aggressive cat will stare at his enemy. When playing or hunting, or if surprised, a cat's pupils will dilate, allowing the maximum amount of light to enter the eye. Cats are crepuscular, meaning they are most active at dawn and dusk, when they will rely on their ability to see movement in low light in order to hunt small prey.

Ears

If a cat is uneasy, he will flick his ears around, remaining alert to any sound that may signify danger. The ears flatten at the first sign of conflict, to protect them from damage in case there's a fight.

Posture

A cat will usually arch his back when he is fearful, to make himself look bigger when trying to scare off an aggressor. An aggressor might arch his back a little, too, to look as large and intimidating as he can.

A scared cat might crouch low when trying to escape a situation, as will a cat who is stalking prey. When you watch a cat hunt or play, you might notice that he wiggles his bottom before pouncing on an object. This helps his eyes to pinpoint the exact position of the prey and helps to ready his body, balance-wise, for the leap that will follow.

Litter box training

The advantage of adopting an adult cat is that he is likely to be fully litter box trained already. But even untrained cats are very easy to teach. Thankfully, cats are very clean creatures, and, if you give them the right materials in the right places, they will pretty much train themselves! Put down a box of litter in a quiet corner of the house (in the cat room you have prepared for him), show it to him, tell him what a good boy he is when he uses it, and usually that's it. Job done!

If he does have accidents, then there's a reason why.

- Is the box too close to his bed or food bowls? Understandably, cats don't like to toilet near where they sleep or eat.

- Perhaps the cat litter isn't pleasant for him to walk on (some cats don't like, for example, the wood-type pellets and prefer a fine-grain litter).

- Maybe there's not enough privacy and he doesn't feel secure to go– perhaps because it's too busy and people are coming and going, or he's being stalked by another cat. So make sure there are plenty of boxes scattered around the house in a multi-cat household, perhaps purchase a covered box, and make sure the boxes are in quiet corners and not busy thoroughfares.

- Is the box clean? If you don't scoop poop promptly and change all the litter regularly, the cat will find a cleaner place to relieve himself—such as a quiet spot behind your sofa.

- If you have an older puss, can he access the box easily? Perhaps he can't get into the covered box or finds it too much of a struggle to go down the stairs to get to it. Have plenty of shallow boxes around the house.

- If he suddenly becomes incontinent, or, despite your best efforts, continues to have accidents, you must get him seen by a vet, as an underlying health problem may be responsible.

- Is the cat scent-marking rather than toileting (see page 79)?.

If your cat does have an accident, it is vital that the area is cleaned thoroughly, as the cat will otherwise be attracted back to the area to repeat his performance! Even if the area smells clean to you, the cat's sensitive nose will pick up any trace of scent. An ordinary household cleaner, even bleach, vinegar, or baking soda, will not do the job. If an area smells of urine, who can blame him for thinking it's a toileting spot? Use a cleaning product made specifically to clean animal urine, and then wipe with water and dry. Do this cleaning routine on a small, unnoticeable part of the surface first, to check that it is safe to continue.

If your cat returns to the area out of habit, then move the furniture around so he can't get to the same spot again. Or try putting a litter box over that spot.

Pregnant women and those with compromised immune systems should always wear gloves to change litter and to clean out the litter box because of the small risk of Toxoplasmosis, an infection caused by a microscopic **parasite**. And of course, everyone should wash their hands after scooping the box!

Outdoors or in?

Outdoors or in?

Think carefully about whether you need to let your cat go outdoors. A cat roaming free outside is inevitably exposed to many dangers—from traffic, from curiosity (which might cause them to be shut in other people's houses, sheds, or garages), from poisons in people's gardens or garbage or cars, or from eating a mouse or rat that has ingested toxins, and from other animals, including other cats, dogs, and wild animals (some of which will eat your cat and all of which will fight if they feel threatened).

We also know that the world is not full of cat lovers, and some people may throw things at your cat, or try to harm him in other ways—especially if he is annoying them. Your neighbors might not appreciate your cat coming onto their property, digging and eliminating in their garden, hanging out on their car or deck, coming up to their windows and doors and upsetting their cats and dogs.

In many municipalities, it is illegal to let your cat roam. While these laws are typically not enforced, if your cat is picked up, you will have to pay a hefty fine to get him back—if you get him back at all. Your cat is your pet and your responsibility, and needs to stay on your property.

Does this mean he can never enjoy the great outdoors? Not at all. What it means is that it's not responsible to simply open the door in the morning, let your cat out, and remind him to be home before dark. Cats should enjoy the great outdoors the same way dogs and toddlers do: in a safely fenced yard, with human supervision.

Humane societies agree that the only way to let a cat out is to first safely cat fence your yard, or to build a secure enclosure in a part of your yard. Cat-safe fencing goes into the ground and curls inward on top, so your cat can't climb the fence and escape. There are also a variety of clever outdoor enclosures (catios!) you can build for a cat, ranging from a simple screened-in porch to an elaborate enclosed playpen.

If your cat is outside in the yard or in an enclosure, always make sure he has access to fresh water and a suitable area away from his resting and play places to eliminate. He'll need both shade and sun, and a way to get safely inside if it starts to rain or if something scares him. (If you're outside with him, as you should be, you are his way to get inside.)

If you do let your cat out in the yard, you'll need to have a way to quickly call him to you. It's really simple to teach a cat to come. Every day, take out the bag of cat treats, shake it until he comes, and then feed him a few treats. The sound of the shaking bag is now his cue to come to you. Do not let your cat out, even into a well-fenced yard, until you know you can reliably call him back to you. Then, use this cue every day to call your cat to you to come inside. This way, coming in doesn't mean the fun is over—it means a treat is coming!

Increasingly, cats are the pets of choice for people who live in cities. If you don't have a yard, does that mean your cat can't go out? He can! Many cats have learned to walk on a leash and harness. You may have even seen cats on a leash in your city. Adult cats who have spent their lives indoors may not enjoy walking on a leash outside—but they also may surprise you! It's worth giving it a try. And if you start them out as kittens, they are likely to love it.

Most cats can slip out of a collar, so you'll need to get a harness or walking jacket that fits the cat properly (they are typically sold in sizes according to the cat's weight). Here's how you train him to go for a walk:

• Start indoors. Leave the harness on the floor for a few days for your cat to smell and play with.

• Then put him into it, feeding plenty of treats as you do. Don't turn this into a struggle; if the cat is upset, stop and try again tomorrow—with even more treats.

• Let your cat wear the harness around the house for a few minutes, then take it off and play with him. Repeat until he is confortable putting it on.

• Put the harness on again and attach the leash. Let him drag the leash around the house for a few minutes (you must supervise to make sure he doesn't get tangled on something). Take it off and play with him. Repeat until he is comfortable.

• When you and your cat are ready to go out, open the door and let your cat sniff around. If you have some stairs or an elevator before you get outdoors, you can use that space as your first leash walk.

• Let the cat choose the direction he walks in; don't expect him to heel like a dog. You can encourage him with occasional treats.

- If you live in a busy street, pick a time when things are quiet and less busy for your cat's walks.

- Pay attention to your cat's body language. He will tell you if he's feeling stressed or scared. Look for flattened ears, body low to the ground, meowing, or nervous tail twitching. If your cat is not having a good time, take him inside.

- Make sure your cat doesn't become an escape artist. Some cats may wait by the door and bolt outside whenever it is opened. Make it clear to your cat that the only time he can go outside is when he is dressed in his harness. Keep a little bowl of cat toys near the door, and throw one into the house just before you open the door; when your cat chases it, you can safely open the door.

Cats who go outdoors have very different vaccination and parasite control needs than do indoor-only cats, so be sure to tell your veterinarian if your cat goes out, even on leash walks.

House cats

Many people keep their cats permanently indoors, with no loss of welfare for the cat. With a house cat, you have to work extra hard to ensure all your puss's needs are met. If he is deprived of opportunities to express his natural behavior—hunting, climbing, scratching, and all the rest—he will become bored and unhappy, and serious behavior problems can result.

Is he sociable? Would he enjoy a feline playmate? A second cat can be a great companion.

Play with him as much as you can throughout the day, using a variety of toys to maintain his interest. Set aside time for regular training sessions, too. Cats are very intelligent and take well to training methods that are based in positive rewards, such as clicker training.

Using his brain will keep him mentally alert—plus it's fun and strengthens the pet/owner bond. Give him work to do by feeding his dry kibble only from food-dispenser toys. These are toys your cat must manipulate to get the food out. There's nothing more natural—or more satisfying—for a cat than working to get his food!

Indoor grass is a must for a house cat. Cats enjoy nibbling grass and it's thought to provide essential roughage to prevent constipation and prevent

hairballs. You can bring in other items from the outdoors as well, such as large sticks and branches with fresh leaves—as long as you know they have not been sprayed with pesticides.

The Find Out More section of this book also contains resources for ways you can make your indoor cat's life more interesting, stimulating, and satisfying.

Common
Behavior
Problems

Common Behavior Problems

Cats are pretty straightforward creatures and rarely have behavioral problems. But if they haven't been raised well and thoroughly socialized, or if their basic needs are not met, problems might develop.

Often it is simply a matter of understanding why the cat is behaving as he is (perhaps he is being destructive due to boredom, for example), and providing him with what he is lacking (in this case, more varied, stimulating play and opportunities to exercise his mind and body). But if you are unable to deal with a problem, do not hesitate to contact an expert, as behavior issues can escalate quickly. The sooner you address the problem, the better! It's a myth that cats can't be trained or change their behavior. Your vet will first check that there is no underlying health issue responsible for the problem, before referring you to a suitable expert—one who is qualified and experienced in dealing with cat behavior in a kind, non-punitive, reward-based manner.

Scratching

Scratching *per se* isn't a problem; it's a necessary feline behavior. A cat needs to scratch to groom his claws (the outer husk is removed through scratch-ing, revealing a new, sharp point beneath), to deposit scent from the footpad (surrounding his territory in his own scent, making it feel familiar and safe to him, as well as communicating to other cats that the area has been staked), and to stretch and exercise his muscles.

Scratching only becomes a problem when it is per-formed at an inappropriate place—the arm of the sofa, for example, instead of on the designated scratching post.

There are several reasons why a cat might be scratching inappropriately.

- Does he have enough posts around the house? If he does, are they in the right locations? Cats often scratch at key strategic points in the home, often by doorways. Try moving his scratching trees/posts around, bringing them close to where he is already choosing to scratch, so he has an alternative to your sofa or bed!

- Do the posts meet his needs? Are they upright, steady, and the right height for your cat?

He should be able to reach and get a full stretch. Sisal or bark are the best coverings—certainly not carpet! If the posts are old, do they need to be recovered? If your cat can't sink his claws into on a post, he could seek an alternative outlet.

- Is it an attention-seeking behavior? Forbidden scratching is a sure way of getting an owner's attention—and once your cat has that, he can lead you to the back door or the food bowl, or get you to play with him, or roll over for a tummy tickle Interrupt inappropriate scratching —and instead encourage him to use posts, giving oodles of attention when he uses the right place!

- Sometimes scratching in a particular place has already become a habit, usually from when he was a kitten. To encourage your cat to scratch where you want, cover the inappropriate surface with a plastic tarp or shower curtain and put an excellent post right next to it. Play with him near the post, making the toy run up and down the post so he touches it. Rub some catnip on the post to make it extra attractive. Praise him when he gets it right!

Tip: To discourage inappropriate scratching, apply double-sided sticky tape to the forbidden areas. He won't like the sensation on his paws and will therefore be more likely to use the scratching post you've provided for him.

- Is he stressed? Is he scratching to immerse himself in his own scent? Will a pheromone diffuser help to calm him?

Unless the cause of stress is obvious (perhaps a new cat has joined your home), it's best to get him checked by a vet, in case there's an underlying medical reason for the anxiety. If he's healthy, the vet might refer you to a behaviorist.

Scent marking

This shouldn't be confused with toileting (eliminating), where the cat will generally squat and empty his bladder. With scent marking, however, the cat usually stands with his tail up, and sprays just a small amount on to a vertical surface, such as a wall, door, or table leg. Occasionally a cat squats to deposit a small amount of urine on to something horizontal, such as a bed, or leaves feces there. In all cases of scent marking, the scent (be it urine or faeces) will be left uncovered, whereas the cat will usually try to cover his waste if toileting.

Scent is an important form of communication between cats and they will often scent mark to mark the boundaries to their territory.

So scent marking is a normal feline behavior—but it's not something we appreciate when it's done in our homes!

A cat might mark indoors to make it smell familiar, if he is feeling insecure. Is there an obvious cause for the behavior—for example, a recent move or a new pet joining the home?

Or are free-roaming cats coming around, making him feel like he has to defend his territory? If there is, then a Feliway diffuser or spray might help to boost his confidence while he settles into his new home or you address the cause of his anxiety.

Does he have enough places of security to which he can retreat if visitors come, children are too noisy, or other pets are too boisterous? Can he be a cat to the full? Can he use all his senses and energy, to scratch, play, hunt, and explore?

Is he feeling insecure due to pain or ill-health? There could be an underlying health issue that needs to be investigated by your vet.

If you cannot find the cause of the stress or you need help to address it, then seek a referral to a behaviorist.

Litter box problems

If your cat is not using the litter box (and you're sure the behavior is not scent marking), then it's a case of starting from scratch and checking all the basics are in place: that you have the right box and cat litter and enough boxes in the right locations. Make sure they are scooped and changed regularly, and that your cat doesn't have a health problem that is responsible for the accidents.

Nervousness

Early socialization is so important for a kitten to grow into a happy, confident adult cat. But if you've adopted a rescue puss, who is already an adult, is it too late? Will you always have a nervous cat? Not necessarily. Cats, like people, have different personalities, depending on their genes, upbringing, and life experiences, and some cats are more outgoing than others. But a nervous cat can be helped to be more confident. Some cats just need a few days, weeks, or months to settle into a home and assess the situation, and all family members, before realizing they are safe and can come out of their shell.

Others need a little more help. Although they might never be totally calm and outgoing, you might be able to boost their confidence with lots of play, some training, and possibly even outdoor walks. Just don't force a timid cat to interact with strangers, and make sure he has places to run and hide if he's feeling stressed out.

Showing him that he can trust you and gently socializing him is also worth trying. Put an indoor crate in a corner of the living room, covered with a blanket and with some familiar bedding inside so it creates a cozy den. Give him tasty treats when he's in the crate, so he learns to associate the place with enjoyable experiences. Ask a cat-loving friend or family member to visit at a pre-arranged time—and make sure the cat is in the living room, with all exit routes blocked, so he cannot escape and avoid the situation. The friend can feed the cat treats right through the door of the crate, if the cat is calm enough to accept them. If not, don't force the issue; just being in the same room as a "stranger" is a good first step. Over time, very gradually, with repeated encounters with cat-friendly visitors, the cat's confidence should grow as he realizes that no harm will come to him.

If you need help devising a program to follow, contact a reputable behaviorist. Remember: a steady, patient approach is best: if you rush, all progress can be lost.

Food

Food

Most cats will eat whatever they are given—although some are certainly fussy, particularly if they got away with it when they were younger, with an owner replacing perfectly fine cat food with succulent chicken or tuna the moment a cat, for whatever reason, isn't interested in finishing his meal that day. It doesn't take long for a canny puss to realize that refusing a meal results in finer fare being offered!

Food—keeping your cat healthy

If you adopt an adult cat, try to discover what food the previous owners or rescue center were feeding. A sudden change in diet can cause diarrhea, and this, together with the stress of a new home and settling in with a new family, can put considerable strain on the body. If you want to change the cat's diet, wait at least a few months, until he's settled, and then do it gradually, over the course of a week to 10 days, replacing a little of the cat's ordinary food with the new type, until, eventually, he's eating only the new food.

Types of diet

There is now a type and flavor of food to suit every taste and budget—and there are even veterinary diets for specific health issues. In a nutshell, there are basically dry and wet foods to choose from. Crunching on the hard kibbles of a dry food can be beneficial to a cat's dental health (as opposed to wet foods that stick to the teeth), and dry foods stay fresh much longer, so they make good snacks for overnight or while you are away at work.

Wet food is smellier, messier but often highly attractive to cats, and is preferable for health reasons. Dry foods are full of carbohydrates, which can lead to obesity. Cats also evolved to get much of their daily water intake from their food.

Wet and dry foods usually come in different lifestage varieties, to meet a cat's changing needs—with kitten, adult, indoor cat, and senior varieties available.

Feeding times

Dry food can be put out in the morning and left throughout the day for the cat to graze on. Follow the amounts recommended on the package, but adjust according to your cat's body condition. Or you can divide his daily amount into a couple of portions, which you put down for him morning and evening. This might be preferable if you have a multi-cat household where one greedy puss might tuck into other cats' meals if not monitored.

Wet food should not be left out all day, as it will spoil. Your cats might appreciate a schedule of wet food morning and evening, and small amounts of dry food for snacking in between.

Water

Fresh drinking water must be available at all times. Some cats prefer running water—many a puss will be found pawing at a dripping tap—and pet drinking fountains are available for such water babies.

Cats don't need milk, and some are lactose intolerant. If yours is, you'll see the result in the litter box.

Grooming

Grooming

Most cats are short haired mixes and require minimal coat care, being perfectly equipped to groom themselves. Their rough tongues brush through the coat, distributing natural oils through it and removing dead hair.

Grooming—keeping your cat looking and feeling good.

But that's not to say they don't need a helping hand. An all-over brushing once a week will help to prevent hairballs as well as minimize the amount of hair that is left around the house on carpets, clothing and furniture. It will also help with the pet-owner bond and give you the chance to look for any parasites in the coat and for any physical changes that need to be investigated by a vet, such as lumps or scratches.

Some breeds need more assistance, though, particularly where humans have interfered with the original cat design. For example, the Persian's coat is now so long and thick that the cat would not be able to keep it in good condition without human help.

A Persian would be a matted mess in a very short time if left to his own devices.

When you buy or adopt your cat, the breeder or shelter should give you specific advice on the care that your cat's coat will need.

Routine

Getting a cat used to grooming when still a kitten is ideal, but it's easy enough to get an adult puss used to being brushed and combed if you simply incorporate it into an ordinary petting session. Stroke him all over and, when he's relaxed and purring, simply begin to brush him gently (keep your grooming tools by your favorite armchair, so they are in easy reach!). Brush for just a couple of minutes, give him a treat, and then simply stroke him with your hand again. Later, try a couple more minutes. Keep sessions short and frequent, and very gradually extend them in terms of time and the areas groomed.

Use the services of a professional groomer if you don't have the time or expertise. If your cat would be stressed by the car journey or visit to a salon, find a groomer who will visit your home.

- Cats don't groom just to keep themselves clean; it also helps to cool a cat in warm weather, with the saliva evaporating from the coat, and distributes oils to waterproof the individual hairs.

- Grooming is an important bonding activity between pet and caregiver—and between friendly cats, too.

- A cat usually grooms when calm and content, but he might also groom as a diversionary behavior or if stressed. A cat that over grooms will need to be seen by a vet, who will refer to a behaviorist if necessary.

- Any change in coat or grooming behavior should be reported to your vet, as hair loss or a change in texture may be indicative of a health issue.

Health

104

Health

Cats are pretty robust, healthy creatures, but there are times when they will need veterinary intervention. The sooner this intervention comes, the better the chances of recovery.

WebMD on cat health issues

Be alert to signs of illness so that you can contact your vet at the earliest opportunity. Look out for any change from your cat's usual healthy condition and normal behavior. If he is sleepier than usual; drinking or eating more or less; if he is grooming more or less; if he is grumpy or less tolerant of being petted... all of these signs can suggest that something is wrong. More obvious signs are the physical changes: perhaps there's a change in the type and frequency of his litter box habits; perhaps there's a change to his coat, his eyes and/or nose are runny, or he is scratching himself. Has he lost or put on weight? Does his breath smell? Have any lumps appeared?

All of these signs can be spotted quickly if you spend time with your pet, and instinct often kicks in, too. "I can't put my finger on it, but my cat just doesn't seem himself" is commonly heard at vet practices around the country, and, from there, the vet can examine the animal for more clues.

Do not ever be tempted to treat the cat yourself. Many drugs intended for humans are highly toxic to cats. A visit to the professionals at the first sign of illness often means a condition can be treated quickly—and more affordably.

Pet insurance is worth exploring, as unexpected vet bills can be difficult to deal with—particularly if, given veterinary advances, specialist treatment is given or a chronic, long-term condition emerges. Do be aware of the different types of policies when researching insurance, as some policies only give 12 months' coverage for each condition.

Vaccinations

With adult cats that have been rescued and where the health history is unknown, most vets advise starting from scratch and treating your adult like a kitten—on the assumption that the cat hasn't had any vaccines. If you do have a complete health record for your cat, then continuing with boosters as needed will suffice.

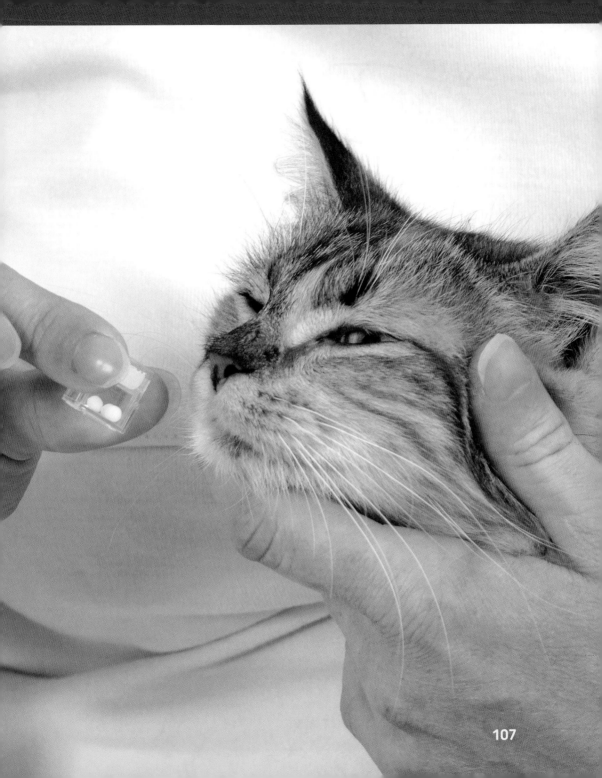

You should research the issue and discuss any concerns with your vet, who will have local knowledge and be able to assess your cat's lifestyle, health and background and help you to come to a decision based on this risk assessment.

Do note that it is important, when adopting an adult rescue of unknown past, to take the cat in for a thorough checkup, including blood work. Vaccinating against feline leukemia, for example, is all well and good, but how do you know that your cat doesn't already have it? Ask the rescue center about its screening policy before you fall in love with a puss. Otherwise, you could end up adopting a cat who could fall ill months later, costing you hundreds of dollars and possible heartbreak—not to mention risking the health of any other cats in the household in the meantime.

Parasites

Ectoparasites live on the skin; endoparasites live inside the body. The most common parasites that affect cats are fleas, ticks, and mites (ectoparasites) and roundworms and tapeworms (endoparasites).

They can all be picked up easily from other cats and/or the environment, so it's important to make regular defleaing and deworming is part of your care routine, particualarly if your cat goes outside. Seek your vet's advice about which products to use (some over-the-counter preparations may not be as effective), and ask about dosage and frequency.

Fleas

Fleas are small, dark, wingless insects that can jump very high—the equivalent to an adult human clearing around 900 feet (274 m)! Once they leap onto your cat, they can go undetected in the fur, laying eggs and reproducing at an alarming rate before you suddenly become aware that you have an infestation—not just on the cat, but in your home, where eggs will have fallen off and hatched in the carpets, gaps in the floorboards, and so on. It's said that for every flea you find on your cat, there will be many more in the home, so as well as treating the cat, it is important, if you find fleas, to remove them from the environment.

Often, you will notice small black specks—the flea dirt—in the coat before noticing the actual fleas. If you groom your cat on a large sheet of white paper, you might notice the specks more easily, as they will fall onto the sheet. Once wetted, the specks will turn red—the blood that the flea has fed on.

Flea treatments for cats include collars, powders, sprays, spot-ons (drops that are applied to the back of the neck), and tablets (which interrupt the flea's breeding cycles). Some people swear by natural repellants, too. It is important to follow your vet's advice, as otherwise a dangerous toxic reaction may occur. Never give your cat flea products made for dogs, as they can be toxic.

Ticks

These can be picked up in long grass. They latch onto the cat's skin and, like fleas, feed on the cat's blood. They swell in size as they feed and eventually drop off. They should be removed carefully, to make sure their contents are not squeezed back into the cat and to also avoid leaving the head/mouthparts embedded in the cat, causing an infection. A tick-removal tool can be bought from your pet shop or vet clinic.

if you are unsure of how to use it, ask your vet to show you how. Do be aware that ticks can spread disease—not only to other animals but sometimes people, so report any adverse effects following a bite to your doctor or vet.

Flea treatments often kill ticks, too; ask your vet for advice.

Mites

Head-shaking and scratching at the ears can be signs that there is something wrong with the ear—either an infection of some sort, or the presence of ear mites. Your vet will diagnose and treat accordingly.

Tiny red insects might be found in the late summer, early autumn called harvest mites or chiggers. These can cause intense itching and a red, spotty reaction.

Biting lice can also be found on feline coats— particularly where the cat is under the weather and has a compromised immune system. The lice are visible with the naked eye, though you might notice a change or loss of coat first.

As ever, seek veterinary advice for a diagnosis and treatment.

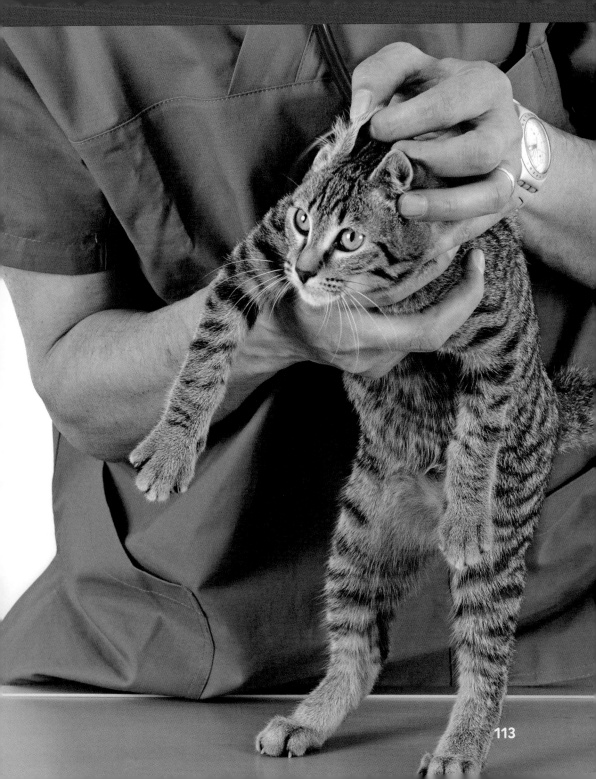

Worms

A cat with fleas can get tapeworms simply by grooming himself. Put simply, flea larvae eat tapeworm eggs. If a cat swallows a flea when grooming, the tapeworm can develop inside him.

You might not know your cat is infected unless the worm burden becomes heavy, resulting in poor health

When you scoop your cat's litter box, you might see segments of the worm in the feces, or you might spot them on the cat's bedding. They will look like small rice grains.

Roundworms can also be a problem, with the eggs passing to other pets or, rarely, people by ingesting egg-infested faeces. Hunting cats are prone to these and to tapeworms, from ingesting rodents that are infected. Kittens are often infected, with the larvae of roundworms passing to them via their mother's milk. A pot-belly, poor condition, and tummy upsets can often indicate a heavy worm burden.

Routine deworming is advised. Frequency and dosage will depend on the preparation used and your cat's lifestyle,. Your vet will give you specific advice according to the treatment he or she recommends.

Fat cats

Some cats know when to stop eating, but others will happily munch their way to obesity. Rescued cats that were once strays, for example, might eat and eat when food is available, storing up food in readiness for a future famine. Other cats are just greedy! Older, less active cats can put on weight simply by being less active. Indoor cats also tend to be less active and therefore put on weight. It's important to make sure that your cat is given lots of opportunity to play and exercise, not only to burn calories but also to avoid boredom. If a cat's only pleasure in life is eating, he'll quickly become obese.

It's not just quantities of food that can cause a cat to put on weight; the type of food can also be inappropriate. Feeding primarily dry food to your cat, for example, isn't going to do his waistline any favors—nor his health.

Your vet will help you monitor your cat's weight and devise a weight-loss program, having first established that there are no underlying health issues causing the problem.

Accidents / first aid

Cats really do seem to have nine lives, managing to get into—and out of—all sorts of scrapes. But that's not to say they are invincible. It's important to be safety-conscious and also to be prepared for emergencies. Keep the cat carrier in an easily accessible place (not hidden at the back of the garage under a ton of unused garden furniture or in far recesses of the closet), so you can find it, put the cat inside and drive to the vet clinic as quickly as possible if your cat needs urgent medical treatment. Post the number of your veterinary clinic on the fridge door, by the phone, or somewhere else that's visible and immediately obvious. Keep a pen and piece of paper close by in case you need to write down the details of the after-hours emergency contact.

There are plenty of good first-aid sites on the Internet that are worth reading, so you are fully prepared for any future emergencies.

Spay and neuter

Neutering involves removing the testes in males and spaying is removing the ovaries and uterus in females. Neutering your cat is essential, to avoid unwanted pregnancies and to protect his or her health. When so many perfectly healthy cats and kittens are being destroyed for want of a home, breeding a litter of random-bred kittens is unforgivable. Even if you have homes for the anticipated kittens, by producing a litter, you will be condemning to death shelter cats that could have been rehomed instead.

Neutering a cat will also prevent spraying in **toms**, howling in **queens** and stop them acquiring sexually transmitted diseases. Toms often fight when competing for a mate, too, and are then at risk of diseases such as calicivirus, FIV and feline leukaemia, for example. Unneutered cats are at increased risk of certain types of cancers, as well.

Reputable shelters will neuter healthy adult rescued cats before they are adopted.

When It's Time to Say Good-bye

When It's Time to Say Good-bye

Sadly, cats do not live as long as humans, and the time will come when your cat dies or has to be put to sleep.

Choosing when to **euthanize** your cat has to be one of the hardest decisions you'll make—and is also one of the most important. You have a duty of care to make sure that your cat has a good quality of life. If he is in pain, with no hope of recovery, your vet will suggest that he is put to sleep, and you should be guided by his or her professional opinion.

The procedure is done by injecting barbiturates into the cat's vein so that he loses consciousness and dies. It is painless for the cat—though terribly painful, in emotional terms, for the devoted owner he leaves behind.

While your cat is young and healthy, it is important to consider what you would like done at the end of his life, as you never know what is around the corner. Perhaps he will die suddenly in an accident, and you will have to make snap decisions, at a highly emotional, stressful time, that you might later regret. Do you want to take the cat's body home to bury in your yard, perhaps under his favorite tree or sun-bathing spot?

Perhaps you want him to be buried in a pet cemetery, so that you can visit him. Perhaps you want him cremated, individually or in a group, and want to scatter his ashes or keep them in a commemorative container. Would you like the vet to visit your home and have him put to sleep in familiar surroundings, or would you prefer to take him to the vet clinic to have it done?

Consider all these aspects when you don't need to, and it will help when the heartbreaking time finally does come.

Finally, if you have never experienced the death of a much-loved pet before, you might be surprised by the strength of your feelings. It is perfectly normal to feel utterly devastated at losing an important member of your family—and it is not unusual for the grief to be overwhelming. Do cry when you need to, talk about your cat with others who knew him, and perhaps seek support from a pet-loss group. Some animal welfare groups also run grief counseling hotlines.

Be assured that, eventually, your tears will be replaced with smiles as you remember your special friend and recall the happy times you shared together.

Find Out More

Books

Bradshaw, John. *Cat Sense*. New York: Basic Books, 2014.

Delzio, Suzanne, and Cindy Ribarich, *Felinestein: Pampering the Genius in Your Cat*. New York: Harper, 1999.

Johnson-Bennett, Pam. *Think Like a Cat*. New York: Penguin, 2011.

Web Sites

indoorpet.osu.edu/cats/
The Indoor Pet Initiative, from Ohio State University Veterinary School, has everything you need to know to keep an indoor cat happy.

www.youtube.com/user/ PositiveCattitudes?feature=mhum
This is the YouTube channel of a very talented cat clicker trainer, to get you started training your cat.

cfa.org and **www.tica.org**
Learn about cat breeds from the Cat Fanciers' Association and The International Cat Association.

# Words to Understand

euthanize to put an animal to death humanely, as relief from serious illness

parasite an organism that takes what it needs from the host it lives on

pedigree the family tree of a purebred animal; a cat with a pedigree is

pheromone a chemical substance produced by an animal that affects the behavior of other animals

toxic poisonous; deadly to living things

tom a male cat who has not been neutered

queen a female cat who has not been spayed

socialization the process of teaching your cat about the world he lives in, so that he does not feel frightened, alarmed, or threatened when he encounters new situations and new experiences

Index